"Why" Stories

A Dolch Classic Basic Reading Book

by Edward W. Dolch and Marguerite P. Dolch

illustrated by Alex Bloch

The Basic Reading Books

The Basic Reading Books are fun reading books that fill the need for easy-to-read stories for the primary grades. The interest appeal of these folktales and legends will encourage independent reading at the early reading levels.

The stories focus on the 95 Common Nouns and the Dolch 220 Basic Sight Vocabulary. Beyond these simple lists, the books use about two or three new words per page.

This series was prepared under the direction and supervision of Edward W. Dolch, Ph.D.

This revision was prepared under the direction and supervision of Eleanor Dolch LaRoy and the Dolch Family Trust.

SRA/McGraw-Hill

A Division of The **McGraw·Hill** Companies

Printed in the United States of America.

Send all inquiries to:
SRA/McGraw-Hill
250 Old Wilson Bridge Road, Suite 310
Worthington, OH 43085

ISBN 0-02-830816-6

1 2 3 4 5 6 7 8 9 0 BUX 04 03 02 01 00 99 98

Table of Contents

Why the Bear Has a Little Tail

One cold day a man went fishing. He cut a hole in the ice on the river. He got many fish. But the man was very cold. So he went away to get warm. He did not take his fish with him, because he was coming back to fish some more. The fish were on the ice by the hole.

A fox came by and saw the fish. He saw how the man got the fish by making a hole in the ice. He took the fish and ran away. And, as he was walking in the woods, he saw a big brown bear. He said to himself, "I think I see how to play a trick on Mr. Bear."

Soon he met Mr. Bear in the woods.

"Look, Mr. Bear," said the fox. "See how many fish I have."

"How did you catch them?" asked the bear, because he did not see how the fox could catch fish.

"I will tell you how to catch fish," said the fox. "Go down to the river and cut a hole in the ice. Sit down on the ice and put your tail into the hole. The fish will take hold of your tail, and then you can pull the fish out of the river."

"Thank you, Mr. Fox, for telling me how to catch fish," said the bear. And the bear went off to the river because he liked very much to eat fish. He was sure he could catch fish the way the fox had told him.

The bear cut a hole in the ice. And then, he sat down on the ice and put his tail into the hole. The ice was very cold. Mr. Bear got colder and colder. The longer he sat on the ice, the colder he got.

At last the bear was so cold that he could not sit on the ice any longer. He started to get up. But he could not get up. His tail was fast in the ice.

The bear pulled and pulled, but he could not get his tail out of the ice.

"Help, help, help," called the bear. "Mr. Fox, come and help me. My tail is fast in the ice."

Mr. Fox was watching from the woods, but the fox did not come to help the bear. That old fox just ran away into the woods to eat his fish.

The bear pulled and pulled. He pulled this way and pulled that way. He pulled and pulled and pulled. At last, his tail broke off.

And that is why, to this very day, the bear has a little tail.

Why the Frog Cries at Night

Once upon a time there was a monkey that lived up in a tree. And this monkey did not like to live all by himself. So one day he went walking in the woods to see if he could find someone to live with.

The monkey saw a frog in the woods. And the frog said to the monkey, "Come and live with me, for I do not like to live all by myself."

"You think just as I do," said the monkey. "It is not good to live all by yourself. So I will come and live with you."

The monkey and the frog lived together for some time. Then, one night it started to rain. It rained all night long. The monkey and the frog were cold. And the frog cried all night long.

In the morning the sun came out. Then, the monkey said to the frog, "We are warm now. But I know how cold we were in the night. Let us work together and make a warm coat today."

But the frog said, "I think that I will sit in the sun. Why should I make a coat today? The sun makes me warm. I like it."

But that night it rained again. It rained all night long. The monkey and the frog were cold. And the frog cried all night long.

In the morning the monkey said, "We must make our coats today, because at night the rain comes. It makes us cold, and we cannot sleep."

But the sun was out, and it was warm. The frog did not want to work. He wanted to sit in the sun. Nothing that the monkey could say would make the frog work. He just sat in the sun all day long.

Now this went on for many, many days. At night the rain came. The frog was cold. He cried all night long. And the monkey could not go to sleep.

In the day the sun came out. It was warm. The frog would not go to work. He just sat in the sun.

"I am not going to live with this frog who will not work," said the monkey to himself. "It is better to live all by myself in the top of a tree."

So the monkey went back to live in the treetops. And there he lives to this day. And what of the frog who would not work?

In the day, he sits in the sun. He is warm, and he sleeps. But at night when it rains, the frog gets cold. Then, he cries, and he cries all night long.

16

How the Rabbit Lost His Tail

Once upon a time, the rabbit had a long tail. And the cat had only a little tail. The cat wanted the long, long tail of the Rabbit.

"I wish that I had that long tail," she said to herself. "The rabbit never uses his long tail, and it would look so pretty on me."

One day when the rabbit went to sleep, the cat got a knife and cut off the rabbit's long tail. She put the tail onto her little tail. Then the cat had a long, long tail, and she was very pleased with herself.

Mr. Rabbit opened his eyes. He saw Mrs. Cat walking around looking at her long tail.

"Don't you think that this long tail looks better on me that it did on you?" asked Mrs. Cat.

"Yes," said Mr. Rabbit. "That long tail looks very pretty on you. I never did have any use for a long tail. I will let you keep it if you will give me your knife."

And so the cat gave the kind rabbit her knife.

The rabbit jumped up and went away laughing and singing, "I lost my long tail, but I got a knife. And now I will get a new tail or something just as good."

Pretty soon the rabbit came to an old man who was making baskets. The old man looked up and saw the rabbit with the knife.

"Oh, Rabbit," said the man, "please let me borrow your knife to help me make my baskets."

"Yes," said the kind rabbit. "I will let you borrow my knife to help you make your baskets." And the rabbit gave his knife to the old man.

But when the old man started to use the knife, the knife broke.

"Look what I have done," cried the old man. "I have broken your new knife."

Then, the rabbit said, "A broken knife is of no use to me. But a broken knife could help you make your baskets. I will let you keep the broken knife if you will give me one of your baskets."

And so the old man gave the rabbit a basket.

The rabbit jumped up and went away, laughing and singing.

"I lost my long tail, but I got a knife. I lost the knife, but I got a basket. And now I will get a new tail or something just as good."

Pretty soon the rabbit came to an old woman who was picking lettuce. But she had so much lettuce that she could not carry it.

"Oh, Rabbit," said the old woman. "Please let me borrow your basket so that I can carry my lettuce."

"Yes," said the kind rabbit. "I will let you borrow my basket so that you can carry your lettuce." And the rabbit gave his basket to the old woman.

But when the old woman put her lettuce into the basket, the basket broke.

"Look what I have done," cried the old woman. "I have broken your new basket."

Then, Mr. Rabbit said, "A broken basket is of no use to me. I will let you keep the broken basket if you will give me some lettuce."

And so the old woman gave the rabbit some lettuce.

The rabbit jumped up and went away, laughing and singing, "I lost my long tail and I got a knife. I lost my knife, and I got a basket. I lost my basket, and I got some lettuce."

Now the rabbit was very tired. So he sat down and ate some lettuce.

"This lettuce is the best thing that I have had," said the rabbit to himself. "I have found something that I like better than my long tail. I have found something that I like better than the knife. I have found something that I like better than the basket. I have found out that I like lettuce.

And from that day to this, no rabbit has had a long tail.

And from that day to this, every rabbit that you can find likes to eat lettuce.

Why the Baby Says "Goo"

There once was an Indian chief who was very brave.

The Indians said their chief was the bravest man of all. They said there was no one like him. They did just what the chief told them to do. And the chief began to think too much of himself.

There was an old Indian grandmother who was told that the chief was thinking too much of himself. She knew that it was not a good thing for an Indian chief to think that there was no one better than he. And so she asked the Indian chief to come to her home.

"Grandmother, I have come to see you. What is it that you wish to tell me?" said the Indian chief.

"I have heard that you are a very brave chief," said the grandmother. "And our people all do just as you say. But there is one who is braver than you. He will not do as you say."

"Grandmother, who is this one?" asked the chief.

"He is called Wasis," said the old grandmother.

"And where is Wasis, grandmother?" asked the chief.

"Look," said the old grandmother. "He is here in my home."

The chief looked. And he saw on the floor of the home a little Indian baby. The baby looked so pretty, and he laughed at the chief.

"Come here to me," said the chief.

But the baby did not come. He only laughed.

Now the people always did just what the chief told them to do. And so the chief said to the baby, "COME HERE TO ME."

But the baby did not come. The baby cried, and he cried. And the chief did not know what to do.

"Grandmother," said the chief, "the people all do what I tell them to do. But the baby will not do what I tell him to do. He will not come to me. He talks back to me."

"The baby is very brave," said the old grandmother. "He talks back to the chief."

"I will overcome him with my dancing," said the chief. And he danced all around the baby. The chief danced, and he danced, and he danced.

Little Wasis watched the chief. He liked the dances.

"Goo, goo, goo," said little Wasis. "Goo, goo, goo."

"The baby is very brave," said the old Grandmother. "He talks back to the chief."

"What is he saying?" asked the chief.

"He says you are to come to him," said the old grandmother.

The baby did not go the chief. The brave chief went to the baby. When a baby says, "Goo, Goo," he wants you to come to him.

Why Turkeys Have Red Eyes

Little Gray Rabbit did not have any mother. He did not have any father. Little Gray Rabbit lived with his old grandmother.

The grandmother rabbit was so old that she could not work very much. And Gray Rabbit was so little that he could not work very much. They did not have much to eat.

One day, they had only a little handful of corn.

"Grandmother," said Little Gray Rabbit, "you are old, and you must have good things to eat. I am going out in the woods. And I will get you something good to eat."

"Little Gray Rabbit," said the old grandmother, "you are too little to go out into the woods. Come and eat this handful of corn."

But Little Gray Rabbit put a big bag on his back and went out into the woods.

By and by, Little Gray Rabbit saw some big turkeys walking and eating.

"Just look at those big turkeys," said Little Gray Rabbit to himself. "How can I get a big turkey for my grandmother?"

Little Gray Rabbit watched the turkeys go around in the grass.

He said to himself, "I must think how I can get those big turkeys into my bag."

Little Gray Rabbit watched for a long time, thinking and thinking. Then, he got up and put grass into his big bag. When the bag was full of grass, Little Gray Rabbit put it upon his back and ran to where the turkeys were walking around and around.

The turkeys looked up.

"Little Gray Rabbit," called the turkeys, "why are you running with a big bag upon your back?"

"I am going to a dance," said Little Gray Rabbit. "I have been asked to sing so that everyone can dance."

"Little Gray Rabbit," called the turkeys, "Come and sing for us. We want to dance too."

"No, no, do not stop me," said Little Gray Rabbit. "I must go and sing for the big dance."

But the turkeys would not let the little Gray Rabbit go. They wanted him to sing for them so that they could dance.

"Very well," said Little Gray Rabbit, "I will sing for you if you will do just what I tell you to do."

The turkeys all said that they would do just what Little Gray Rabbit told them to do.

"When I sing," said Little Gray Rabbit, "you must shut your eyes and dance around me." And then, Little Gray Rabbit started to sing.

"Turkeys dance, Turkeys dance,
Around and around they go.
Around and around they go.
Turkeys dance, Turkeys dance,
Eyes shut, eyes shut.
Do not look, do not look.
Turkeys dance, Turkeys dance.
If you look, your eyes turn red.
If you look, your eyes turn red."

The turkeys shut their eyes. They danced around and around Little Gray Rabbit. And as they danced around and around, Little Gray Rabbit put some of them into his big bag.

Pretty soon one of the turkeys opened his eyes. When he saw what Little Gray Rabbit was doing, he called, "Open your eyes. Open your eyes. The rabbit is putting us into his bag."

The turkeys opened their eyes. But Little Gray Rabbit picked up his bag and ran away as fast as he could go.

When Little Gray Rabbit got home, he gave the bag of turkeys to his grandmother.

"Now we will have something good to eat," said Little Gray Rabbit. "I will go and get some wood to make a fire. But, Grandmother, do not open the bag."

The old grandmother looked at the bag a long time. She wanted to know what was in the bag. And then she opened the bag. The turkeys jumped out. The old grandmother got hold of the legs of one turkey. But the other turkeys all got away.

And when Little Gray Rabbit got home with the wood to make the fire, he found that his grandmother had only one turkey.

"What have you done, Grandmother?" cried Little Gray Rabbit.

"I let the turkeys out of the bag," said the old Grandmother. "Now we have only one turkey to eat."

And do you know from that time to this, all turkeys have red eyes. People say that it is because the turkeys opened their eyes when Little Gray Rabbit was singing to them.

"Turkeys dance, Turkeys dance,
Around and around they go,
Around and around they go.
Turkeys dance, Turkeys dance,
Eyes shut, eyes shut.
Do not look, do not look.
Turkeys dance. Turkeys dance.
If you look, your eyes turn red
If you look, your eyes turn red."

Why the Turtle Has a Shell on Its Back

One day the water buffalo said to the turtle, "Come with me, I know where we can find some bananas to eat."

So the water buffalo and the turtle went down to the master's garden, which was by the water. The water buffalo, who is very big, picked the bananas and gave some to the turtle, who is very small.

Some people who were working in the master's garden not far away saw the water buffalo and turtle eating the bananas. They went and told the master.

"Go," said the master. "Get the water buffalo and the turtle out of my garden. Bring them to me."

Then all the people went out to get the water buffalo and the turtle who were eating the bananas in their master's garden.

When the water buffalo and the turtle saw the people coming, the turtle called out, "Do not hurt us. The master said that we may have all the bananas that we want."

The people said that this was not so.

"We are going to take you to the master," said the people. "And he is going to eat you because you are eating his bananas."

Then, the water buffalo, who is very big, ran away as fast as he could go. And the people could not get him.

But the turtle, who is very small, could not get away.

When the master saw the turtle, he said, "Pretty soon we will all have turtle soup. But first let us go to the garden and get some good things to put into our turtle soup."

And so they put the turtle in a box, and the master and all of his people went down to the garden by the water to get some good things to put into the turtle soup. And only the children were there at the house to watch the turtle.

The turtle called to the children. "Good, kind children, come and let me out so that I can play with you."

The children did not know what to do.

"Please let me out so that I can play with you," said the turtle. "You will laugh at my funny walk."

Then, the children let the turtle out of the box. The turtle walked away, and the children laughed at his funny walk.

"Come back to us," called the children. And the turtle walked back to the children.

And then the turtle said to the children, "I like to see pretty things. Show me your things."

The children went into the house and got a big bowl. In the big bowl there were many pretty shells.

The children put the pretty shells around the turtle's head. They put the pretty shells around the turtle's legs. And then they put the big bowl on the turtle's back. And how the children laughed.

Just then the master called, and the turtle saw that the master and the people were all coming back to the house. The turtle walked away as fast as he could go. He let go of the little shells on his head and legs. But the big bowl was on his back. He went in the grass, and the children could not see him.

"Come, come," cried the children. "The turtle is running away."

But the turtle got to the water, and he went down under it.

The people ran to the water, and they called to the turtle, "Come and show yourself to us."

The turtle put his head out of the water and looked at the people.

The people threw big sticks at the turtle. But the sticks could not hurt the turtle because the big bowl was on his back.

And after that, the turtle always has a big bowl upon his back. We call it the turtle's shell. The turtle puts his head and his legs and his tail all inside his shell. And then no one can hurt him.

The Tail of the Fox

There was an old woman who lived on a farm. She had some cows and she had some sheep. But she had no one to look after her cows and her sheep. And so one day she said to herself, " I am going to find someone who will look after my cows and my sheep for me."

The old woman walked down the road. She looked everywhere. But she could not find anyone to take care of her animals. Pretty soon she saw a big brown bear.

"Where are you going, Grandmother?" asked the bear.

"I want to find someone who will look after my cows and my sheep for me," said the old woman.

"I will look after your cows and your sheep for you," said the big brown bear.

"Can you call my animals when it is time to bring them home?" asked the old woman.

"Oh, yes," said the bear.

"Show me how you would call my animals," said the old woman.

Then, the bear tried to show the old woman how he would call her animals. But the bear could only growl, because he had always growled.

"No, no, no," said the old woman. "My cows and my sheep would all run away when they heard you."

Then, the old woman went on down the road. Pretty soon she saw a wolf.

"Where are you going, Grandmother?" asked the wolf.

"I want to find someone who will look after my cows and my sheep for me," said the old woman.

"I will look after your cows and your sheep for you," said the wolf.

"Can you call my animals when it is time to bring them home?" asked the old woman.

"Oh, yes," said the wolf.

"Show me how you will call my animals," said the old woman.

Then, the wolf tried to show the old woman how he would call her animals. The wolf put his nose up, and he called, and he called.

"No, No, No," said the old woman. "My cows and my sheep would all run away when they heard you."

Then the old woman went on down the road. Pretty soon she saw a fox.

"Where are you going, Grandmother?" asked the fox.

The old woman was very tired, and so she said to the fox, "I am going home now, because I cannot find anyone to look after my cows and my sheep for me. The bear was kind and said that he would look after them. But he growls so that my animals would run away. The wolf was kind and said that he would look after my cows and my sheep for me. But when he calls, my animals would run away. I do not know what to do, for I am too old to look after my cows and my sheep."

"No, Grandmother, you are not too old," said the fox. "But I should like to work for you if you will let me."

"Can you call my animals when it is time to bring them home?" asked the old woman.

"Oh, yes," said the fox.

"Show me how you will call my animals," said the old woman.

Then, the fox showed the old woman how he would call her animals.

"That is good," said the old woman. "I know that my cows and my sheep will like you."

"And I know that I shall like them," said the fox, and he laughed to himself.

"Come home with me," said the old woman. "And I will show you how to look after my animals."

And so the fox looked after the cows and the sheep for the old woman. But every day one of the cows or one of the sheep was gone.

The old woman said, "Where is my cow?" or "Where is my sheep?"

First, the fox said that a bear came out of the woods. He killed a cow and ate it. Then, the fox said that a wolf came out of the woods. He killed a sheep and ate it.

The old woman did not know what to do.

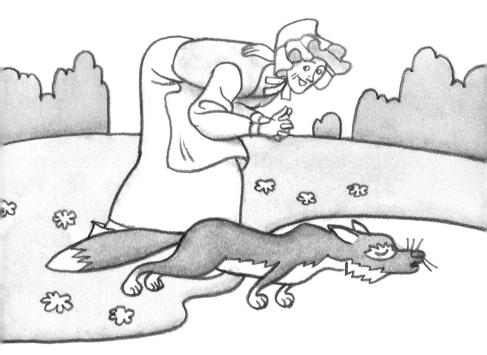

"Mr. Fox," she said, "Why don't you look after my cows and my sheep better?"

"Grandmother, Grandmother," said the fox. "All day long I run up and down looking after the cows and the sheep. I get so tired that I must have gone to sleep."

"Do not go to sleep again," said the old woman. "You must not let my animals be killed."

That day the old woman got to thinking.

"That fox must be very tired from looking after my animals," she said to herself. "I will take him a drink of milk."

But, when she got to where her cows and her sheep were, she saw that the fox going to kill a sheep. Then, the old woman knew that it was the fox who had killed her animals.

The fox saw the old woman and started to run away.

The old woman had nothing with her but the milk. So she threw the milk at the fox.

Some of the milk got on the end of his tail. And from that day to this, the end of the fox's tail has been white.

a
after
again
all
always
am
an
and
animals
any
anyone
are
around
as
asked
at
ate
away
baby
back
bag
bananas
basket
baskets
be
bear
because
been
began
best
better
big
borrow
bowl
box
brave
braver

bravest
bring
broke
broken
brown
buffalo
but
by
call
called
calls
came
can
cannot
care
carry
cat
catch
chief
children
coat
coats
cold
colder
come
comes
coming
corn
could
cow
cows
cried
cries
cut
dance
danced
dances

dancing
day
days
did
do
doing
done
don't
down
drink
eat
eating
end
every
everyone
everywhere
eyes
far
farm
fast
father
find
fire
first
fish
fishing
floor
for
found
fox
fox's
frog
from
full
funny
garden
gave

get
gets
give
go
going
gone
goo
good
got
grandmother
grass
gray
growl
growled
growls
had
handful
has
have
he
head
heard
help
her
here
herself
him
himself
his
hold
hole
home
house
how
hurt
I
ice

if
in
Indian
Indians
inside
into
is
it
its
jumped
just
keep
kill
killed
kind
knew
knife
know
last
laugh
laughed
laughing
legs
let
lettuce
like
liked
likes
little
live
lived
lives
long
longer
look
looked
looking

looks
lost
make
makes
making
man
many
master
master's
may
me
met
milk
monkey
more
morning
mother
Mr.
Mrs.
much
must
my
myself
never
new
night
no
nose
not
nothing
now
of
off
oh
old
on
once

one	saying
only	says
onto	see
open	shall
opened	she
or	sheep
other	shell
our	shells
out	should
overcome	show
people	showed
picked	shut
picking	sing
play	singing
please	sit
pleased	sits
pretty	sleep
pull	sleeps
pulled	small
put	so
puts	some
putting	someone
rabbit	something
rabbit's	soon
rain	soup
rained	started
rains	sticks
ran	stop
red	sun
river	sure
road	tail
run	take
running	talks
said	tell
sat	telling
saw	than
say	thank

that
the
their
them
then
there
they
thing
things
think
thinking
this
those
threw
time
tired
to
today
together
told
too
took
top
tops
tree
treetops
trick
tried
turkey
turkeys
turn
turtle
turtle's
under
up
upon
us

use
uses
very
walk
walked
walking
want
wanted
wants
warm
was
Wasis
watch
watched
watching
water
way
we
well
went
were
what
when
where
which
white
who
why
will
wish
with
wolf
woman
wood
woods
work
working

would
yes
you
your
yourself